THE PARADIGM OF MAN AND EARTH

THOMAS ROBINSON

DIVINE WORKS PUBLISHING, LLC.
ROYAL PALM BEACH, FLORIDA

© 2024 THOMAS ROBINSON
ALL RIGHTS RESERVED

All rights reserved. No part of this publication may be reproduced, stored in a retrieval system, or transmitted in any form or by any means, electronic, mechanical, photocopying, recording or otherwise without the prior permission of the publisher or in accordance with the provisions of the Copyright, Designs, and Patents Act 1988 or under the terms of any license permitting limited copying issued by the Copyright Licensing Agency.

The views expressed in this work are solely those of the author and do not necessarily reflect the views of the publisher. The publisher hereby disclaims any responsibility for them.

ISBN-13: 978-1-949105-58-2 (paperback)
ISBN-13: 978-1-949105-66-7 (eBook)

First Edition Published: 05/28/2024
Printed in the United States

Divine Works Publishing books are available at special discounts when purchased in quantity for premiums and promotions and for educational and fundraising use. For details, contact *books@divineworkspublishing.com* or call the phone number listed below.

Published by:
Divine Works Publishing
Royal Palm Beach, Florida USA
www.DivineWorksPublishing.com
561-990-BOOK (2665)

DEDICATION

This book is dedicated to all believers who are seeking God's deep truths, hidden mysteries, and spiritual revelations, for the purpose of growing in the knowledge of Him—at one and the same time growing in the knowledge of His creation.

"Then God said,

"Let Us make man in Our image,

according to Our likeness;

let them have dominion

over the fish of the sea,

over the birds of the air,

and over the cattle,

over [g]all the earth"

and over every creeping thing

that creeps on the earth."

–Genesis 1:26

CONTENTS

INTRODUCTION | 1
THE BEGINNING | 3
THE CONDITION OF MAN | 9
DARKNESS | 13
CREATION PERMITTING GOD | 17
A SEPARATION | 25
FRUITFUL | 33
EXPOSURE | 49
THE PRAYER | 53

ABOUT THE AUTHOR | 57

ACKNOWLEDGMENTS

*I would like to extend my deepest gratitude
to those who have supported and inspired me throughout
the journey of writing this book.*

First and foremost, I wish to thank my beloved wife, Dr. Teresa Robinson, for her unwavering support and encouragement. Your love and dedication have been a constant source of strength.

To Pastor Harold McCoy, my father-in-law and mentor, your wisdom and guidance have been invaluable to me. Thank you for being a pillar of support.

A special thanks to my friend and associate, Apostle Ricky Graves, and the congregation of Spirit and Truth Church in Cocoa, Florida. Your faith and fellowship have been a true blessing.

I am also deeply grateful to the wonderful people of Victory International Praise Ministries in Melbourne, Florida. Your warmth and support have profoundly impacted my life.

To Pastor C.H. Carter of New Hope Deliverance Temple in Cocoa, Florida, thank you for the significant impact you have made on our lives. Your teachings and compassion have been a source of great inspiration.

Lastly, my heartfelt appreciation to Dr. Lord M. Hunt of West Palm Beach, Florida. The early days spent sitting at your feet and learning about the things of God were incredibly formative and enriching.

*Thank you all for your remarkable contributions and support.
This book would not have been possible without you.*

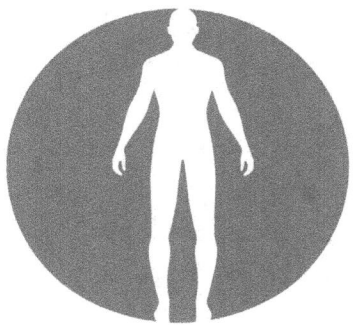

INTRODUCTION

I extend my heartfelt gratitude for purchasing my book and ask that you would indulge me for a moment to pray a prayer from Ephesians Chapter 1, that the GOD of my LORD JESUS CHRIST, the FATHER of Glory, may grant you a Spirit of Wisdom and Revelation in the knowledge of HIM. May the veil be lifted from the eyes of your understanding, illuminating the depth of HIS calling, the boundless riches of HIS inheritance among the saints, and the unmatched power bestowed upon those who bear the name of Jesus. Amen!

In the Genesis account, it is written that in the beginning, GOD created the heavens and the earth. The earth was formless and desolate, shrouded in darkness, and the SPIRIT of GOD hovered over the deep waters.

Imagine, if you will, that you are the very essence whom GOD speaks of, inhabiting this transient world as described in Genesis 1:1-14. Picture yourself, formless and submerged in darkness.

Contemplate the notion that the SPIRIT OF GOD continues to move across the waters (symbolic of His word), stirring a message designed specifically for you. This divine revelation, uttered by a chosen vessel, a herald of GOD, aims to illuminate and save you.

Having captured your attention, let us delve into the purpose behind why GOD concealed your existence at the genesis of time!

Now, what if I told you that you are the one that GOD is speaking of, besides this planet you're temporarily living on, in Gen 1:1-14.

What if I told you that you were without form and void and filled with darkness.

What if I told you that the SPIRIT OF GOD is still moving across the face of the waters (water being symbolic of the word of GOD), stirring up a word, tailor made just for you, activated and released from a vessel; a willing preacher, sent by GOD—that you might be enlightened and saved.

Now that I have your attention, let's explore why GOD hid *you* in the beginning of the book of Genesis and spoke about *your* beginning!

CHAPTER 1

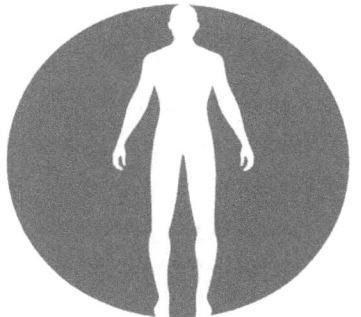

THE BEGINNING

At the age of around 31, I found myself walking through the Merritt Square Mall in Merritt Island, Florida. It was there that I encountered Owen Ward Sr., a prophet sent by God. At the time, I had no idea he was a prophet. He approached me and asked if he could have a word with me. Agreeing, I allowed him to take me aside. That's when he declared, "Thus says the Lord, you are going to preach the gospel. You are going to do television and radio, and many other things." He finished by instructing me to study Genesis 1.

Little did I know at the time that all the things he spoke of would come to pass. I worked the night shift at the Kennedy Space Center, dedicating my quiet hours to reading through the Bible once a year. But when I began studying Genesis 1, after the encounter with Owen Ward Sr., it was as if a veil had been lifted. I started seeing from God's perspective, understanding His love for mankind and how He had carefully woven this love into the beginning of the Bible.

Genesis 1:1 in the NIV translation reads, *"In the beginning God created the heavens and the earth."* This got me thinking maybe David and his deep understanding (revelation of God) realized the connection between man and the earth or the paradigm. Yet, he was prompt to inquire of God. In Psalm 8:3-8, David asks God, *"When I consider your heavens, the work of your fingers, the moon and the stars, which you have set in place, what is mankind that you are mindful of them, human beings that you care for? You have made them a little lower than the angels and crowned them with glory and honor. You made them rulers over the works of your hands; you put everything under their feet: all flocks and herds, and the animals of the wild, the birds in the sky, and the fish in the sea, all that swim the paths of the seas."*

In prophetic language, David is essentially questioning why God, the creator of the vast universe, would care about us. He acknowledges that God not only visits and cares for us, but He also bestows honor and authority upon humans. This realization leads me to believe that mankind holds a special place in God's heart, given that He also demonstrates great mindfulness toward the heavens, naming and differentiating each planet.

Psalm 147:4-5 declares, *"He determines the number of the stars and calls them each by name. Great is our Lord and mighty in power; his understanding has no limit."* Isaiah 40:26 further supports this, stating, *"Lift up your eyes on high and see: who created these? He who brings out their host by number, calling them all by name; by the greatness of his might and because he is strong in power, not one is missing."*

It is intriguing to consider that Genesis 1:1 specifically mentions that God created both the heavens and the earth at the beginning. Paul further expounds on the concept of multiple heavens in 2 Corinthians, referencing the third heaven as the celestial kingdom where God's throne resides.

The second heaven, or the universe mentioned by David in his prayer, is an expanding cosmos that is rapidly expanding at a rate of 41.9 miles per second per mega parsec. It is home to countless galaxies, stars, and star systems, our universe is currently about 95 billion light years across.*

---

*http://science.nasa.gov, *Mystery of the Universe's Expansion rate Widens with New Hubble Data*, Published: April 25, 2019

Isaiah 40:12, according to the NLT translation, reveals that God *"has measured off the heavens with his fingers."* What is the span of GOD'S hand to mark off the heavens? A span means the distance of your hand between the little finger and the thumb when the hand is stretched out, open palm, fingers not touching. There is not a lot of distance there, at least for us. The LORD is saying HE can fit the universe in the span of his hand.

So now if the universe is limited to the span of the CREATOR'S hand and it (the universe) is still expanding, that could only mean that it has not yet grown large enough to fill the span (distance) of HIS hand between the thumb and the little finger and will continue to expand until it does. Of course, we shouldn't forget the significance of the first heaven, the breathtaking blue sky we marvel at from the surface of the Earth. Psalm 147:8 shares, *"Who covereth the heaven with clouds, who prepareth rain for the earth, Who maketh grass to grow upon the mountains."*

Furthermore, Genesis 1:1 states that God created the Earth. It is important to remember that God often speaks figuratively, symbolically, and in mysteries, parables, pictures, types, and patterns. He enjoys hiding truths within His Word. Even Jesus frequently spoke in parables, which often led people to question Him.

Allow me to offer an example from 2 Corinthians where believers are portrayed as earthen vessels or jars holding treasure, something of great value. In 2 Corinthians 4:7 (KJV), it says, *"But we have this treasure in earthen vessels, that the excellency of the power may be of God, and not of us."* Paul intends to convey that as born-again believers, we carry the Spirit of God, the message of Jesus, and the glory of God within us.

Genesis 2:7 (KJV) demonstrates this again, as it recounts how *"the Lord God formed man of the dust of the ground."* It becomes clear that we are the earthen vessels Paul refers to. Just as God created man from the dust of the ground, everything else He created on Earth originated from the same source.

Numerous chemical substances found in the Earth can also be found within man. I began to realize that God, who loves to conceal aspects of His character and creation (which includes man made in His image), was speaking of planet Earth but also paradigmatically He's referencing mankind, and the state (condition) of man in Genesis chapter 1.

Let's delve a little deeper into this topic by examining verse 2 of Genesis 1. It states that the Earth was without form and void, covered by frozen waters, empty, and dark. In reality, the Earth did not start off in such a state. Throughout Genesis 1, God saw that His creation was good (Genesis 1:4, 10, 12, 18, 21, 25). On the sixth day, after creating humanity, God saw that it was very good (Genesis 1:31).

So, what happened between verses 1 and 2 of Genesis 1 that caused the Earth to become empty, frozen, without form, and darkened? In Genesis 1:28, God instructs Adam and Eve to replenish, or refill, the Earth. By understanding the definition of these two words, "replenish or refill" which mean to *replace*, we can take away that God wanted to replace something. This implies replacing something existent on the Earth before it became empty and void—a flourishing planet teeming with life, trees, and vegetation.

The presence of dinosaur bones further supports this notion. These fossils reveal that life existed on Earth prior to it becoming a desolate, formless, and dark place. According to the Bible, Satan led a rebellion with one-third of the angels in the third heaven but was ultimately defeated and cast down to Earth. His nature is to kill, steal, and destroy, as described in John 10:10. Consequently, Earth fell victim to his destructive tendencies, leading to its bleak condition.

Surprisingly, science and archaeology unintentionally corroborate many aspects mentioned in the Bible. Researchers have discovered evidence indicating that large asteroids impacting Earth caused the demise of dinosaurs and other life forms. They suggest that dust clouds from these collisions filled the sky, blocking the Sun's heat and causing a dramatic drop in temperature. Additionally, the mass and speed of these asteroids resulted in rising ocean levels and consequent flooding, turning Earth into a frozen wasteland devoid of life.

In my personal belief, nothing occurs in the natural realm unless it is first initiated in the spiritual realm. I am convinced that when Satan was cast down to Earth, as described in Luke 10:18 and Revelations 12:4, this spiritual event manifested in the natural dimension as large asteroids striking the planet, leading to immense destruction. In the Greek translation asteroids mean starry or star-like.

Jesus described in Luke 10:18, Satan fell *"like lightning,"* which can be understood as a metaphor for the asteroids streaking across the sky.

In Revelation 12:4, it is said that Satan's tail swept a third of the stars from the sky, tossing them to the Earth. The Bible describes the fall of satan as and the 1/3 of angels from a natural perspective. There was a falling in the spirit realm (parent realm) and the natural realm appearing to look like asteroids and meteorites entering the atmosphere and burning up, streaking across the sky like lightning. Today we call them falling stars, just as Rev 12:4 speaks symbolically of them being as stars.

These "falling stars" can be seen as the fallen angels accompanying Satan in his descent, appearing to us as asteroids or meteorites entering the atmosphere and burning up.

Though scientists argue that these asteroid impacts occurred thousands or even millions of years apart, we must remember that time operates differently in the spiritual realm. As the scripture in 2 Peter 3:8 reminds us, for the Lord, one day is as a thousand years, and a thousand years as one day. The concept of time in the parent realm, or the spirit realm, cannot be constrained by human calculations.

Consider the aftermath of Adam's sin. Not only did he experience a spiritual fall, but this decline also manifested in his physical existence. Aging and mortality became part of the human experience. In a similar manner, the Earth itself was affected by Satan's casting down, resulting in a state of disorder, emptiness, and darkness.

Before we come to know God, we exist in a state of spiritual death, devoid of godly knowledge. Our form is lost, and we are empty of God. In the next chapter, we will delve deeper into this topic.

I firmly believe that science, in many aspects, validates the teachings of the Bible, often in ways that scientists and archaeologists may not

THE PARADIGM OF MAN AND EARTH

fully realize themselves. The intricate relationship between science and faith is a fascinating and ongoing exploration.

NOTES

CHAPTER 2

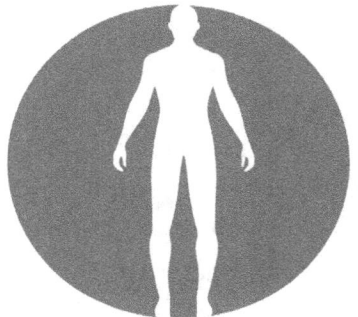

THE CONDITION OF MAN

Now the earth was formless and empty, darkness was over the surface of the deep, and the SPIRIT of GOD was hovering over the waters. –Genesis 1:2

Let us reaffirm together that the earth did not begin in a state of chaos, just as man did not begin in sin. The earth did not lack form from the start; it transformed into that. It became formless, dark, and void. Similarly, man did not exist devoid of the glorious reflection of GOD. Adam began his journey in a unique manner, perfectly fashioned, and untouched by sin. GOD designed the Earth to have a specific size, shape and form and to not be formless. God's original design for man was to have the form of God and to not be without that form. Allow me now to draw a parallel between the state of man and that of the earth.

Man created in the very image of GOD, was adorned with the radiant glory of the divine. Imagine the awe-inspiring sight of Adam and Eve, their countenance reflecting the brilliance of their Creator. Wow! Can you imagine how Adam and Eve must have looked? They possessed a godly form, an embodiment of celestial beauty.

THE PARADIGM OF MAN AND EARTH

As stated in Genesis 1:26, GOD proclaimed, *"Let us make mankind in our image, in our likeness."* Indeed, they were fashioned in the image of GOD, destined to bear His resemblance.

Genesis 2:25 reveals that Adam and Eve dwelt in a state of nakedness, unashamed and unfettered. But how could this be? The answer lies in their raiment of glory, the magnificent covering provided by GOD. So, when GOD showed up in Genesis chapter 3 seeking Adam and Eve, HE was looking for what was in and on HIM; LIGHT and SPLENDOR—he sought attributes of HIS GLORY.

However, once sin crept into their existence, a radical transformation occurred. Genesis 3 states that when Adam and Eve sinned by eating the forbidden fruit that they *fell* from their original state, suddenly becoming aware of their nakedness and concealing themselves with fig leaves. The New International Version of Genesis 3:7 states, *"Then the eyes of both of them were opened, and they realized they were naked; so they sewed fig leaves together and made coverings for themselves."*

Before sin tainted their lives, they communicated openly with GOD, walking side by side without fear or shame. Adam basked in the divine presence, undaunted by any sense of inadequacy. But once sin entered the picture, they recoiled and hid from their Creator.

Adam and Eve were once clothed with the resplendence of light for the very glory of GOD enveloped them.

At their creation, Adam and Eve were perfect. Nevertheless, their fall from grace, prompted by their disobedience and temptation, led to the stripping away of that glorious covering. They suddenly found themselves exposed, consumed by a sense of guilt, fear, and vulnerability.

As we read in Genesis 3:9-11, Adam and Eve's degeneration became evident. With time, humanity gradually lost touch with the knowledge of the true and living GOD. The result is apparent in the world around us today, as many have conformed themselves to the patterns and ways of this world, forsaking the divine likeness they were created to bear.

Romans 12:2, instructs us not to conform to the mold of this world, *"Do not conform to the pattern of this world, but be transformed by the renewing of your mind."*

As the Psalmist proclaims in Psalm 51:5, ***"Behold, I was shapen in iniquity, and in sin did my mother conceive me."*** We find solace in knowing that our FATHER has redeemed us through CHRIST JESUS, desiring that JESUS be formed within us. Galatians 4:19 declares, ***"My dear children, for whom I am again in the pains of childbirth until CHRIST is formed in you."***

The present state of mankind finds itself ensnared by sin, shaped by its iniquities and recklessly conforming to the world's patterns. Their minds are void of godly knowledge. But fear not, for the path to redemption lies before us, as JESUS yearns to take shape within each of us, guiding us back into the glorious image we were originally intended to bear.

NOTES

CHAPTER 3

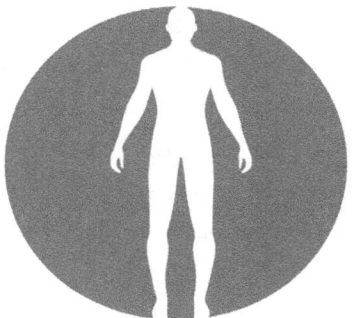

DARKNESS

"darkness was on the face of the deep,"
—Genesis 1:2.

This spiritual darkness caused by the enemy of God, was not merely the absence of light, but a profound spiritual obscurity, a shroud cast by the adversary of divinity. The state of man became darkened just as darkness was upon the face of the deep. Not only was this a natural darkness but also a spiritual darkness. God does not have a problem with darkness, a natural darkness that is. God himself created the day and the night.

> *And God called the light Day, and the darkness he called Night. And the evening and the morning were the first day.*
> *—Genesis 1:5 KJV*

As human population increased upon the face of the Earth, Genesis 6 retells how great wickedness, another way of saying darkness, was upon the earth. The LORD saw how great the wickedness of the human race had become on the earth, and that every inclination of the thoughts of the human heart was only evil all the time.

The LORD saw how great the wickedness of the human race had become on the earth, and that every inclination of the thoughts of the human heart was only evil all the time (Genesis 6:5).

The Bible also tells us that the eyes of man's understanding were darkened, and the spirit of man was darkened, too. Adam and Eve began to die spiritually, and their minds were darkened to the knowledge of God. They were separated from the life of God, in turn the human intellect, once luminous with divine understanding, became obscured; veiled by the ignorance born of hardened hearts.

They are darkened in their understanding and separated from the life of GOD because of the ignorance that is in them due to the hardening of their hearts. –Ephesians 4:18

But God, being the awesome, all-powerful, and loving God that He is, did not leave the earth in a ruined and darkened state. He was not going to allow man to stay in a sinful, degenerate, and darkened state. Just as God rescued the earth from its darkness, He would rescue mankind from its darkness through the birth, life, death, burial, and resurrection of our Lord and Savior Jesus Christ.

In Genesis, the Bible states that the Spirit of God moved upon the face of the water, waiting for a word to be spoken to begin the restoration of the earth. Notice, the SPIRIT OF GOD was moving, sent (authorized) by the FATHER. We see an example in the Bible in the book of John 14 where the HOLY SPIRIT is sent.

But the Comforter, which is the HOLY GHOST, whom the FATHER will SEND in my name, HE shall teach you all things, and bring all things to your remembrance, whatsoever I have said. -John.14:26

The Holy Spirit only puts its power upon the word that is released from the third heaven throne room. We should be mindful of this when preaching the gospel, that the Holy Spirit empowers words that are from the third heaven only––the mind of God, those spoken by the Son Jesus Christ.

I like to say a word that has weight upon it. The weight of the HOLY SPIRIT. When it has been activated, empowered (full of life) by the SPIRIT of the LORD GOD, it will run up out of our belly like JESUS spoke of in the book of John.

> *He that believeth on ME, as the scripture hath said, out of his belly shall flow rivers of living water. –John 7:38 KJV*

This authorized word does not come back void, (empty) but accomplishes that which it was sent to do.

So shall My word be that goes forth from MY mouth; It shall not return to ME void, But it shall accomplish what I please, And it shall prosper in the thing for which I sent it. -Isaiah 55:11 nkjv

We see Peter preaching an activated and empowered word in the book of Acts and about 3,000 were saved (Acts 2:41). Later we read that the number of believers grew to 5,000 (Acts 4:4). I believe the HOLY SPIRIT here is letting us see the numbers and the increase resulting from that which has been empowered from on high.

We can tie this understanding of activation and authority to when God spoke the words "Let there be light!"

> *And GOD said, "Let there be light," and there was light. GOD saw that the light was good, and HE separated the light from the darkness. –Genesis 1:3-4 NIV*

Keep in mind what I shared earlier: GOD doesn't have a problem with night, HE created day and night. This darkness was a spiritual darkness. One of the manifestations of God's glory is light, and everything that we need is in His glory. The Bible says, "And my God shall supply all your needs according to His riches in glory by Christ Jesus" -Phillipians 4:19. The dark, formless, and empty earth needed light, just like this dark, empty and dying world needed light.

*The people who walked in darkness have seen a great light;
those who dwelt in a land of deep darkness,
on them has light shone. –Isaiah 9:2*

*The people dwelling in darkness have seen a great light, and
for those dwelling in the region and shadow of death, on them a
light has dawned. –Matthew 4:16*

To open their eyes, and to turn them from darkness to light, and from the power of Satan unto God, that they may receive forgiveness of sins, and inheritance among them which are sanctified by faith that is in me—Acts 26:18.

Again Jesus spoke to them, saying, *"I am the light of the world. Whoever follows me will not walk in darkness, but will have the light of life." –John 8:12*

Notice, Isaiah stated that they *walked* in darkness—spiritual darkness.

Similarly, Matthew said that they *dwelt* in darkness—spiritual darkness.

The book of Acts clearly was saying that they could turn from *it*, meaning spiritual darkness, Because of the LIGHT, the GLORIOUS LIGHT of GOD.

Christ said in the book of St. John, I am the LIGHT of the world. If we (mankind) would follow CHRIST, we wouldn't have to walk in darkness, dwell in darkness, nor grope blindly in darkness.

*They grope in the dark without light, And He makes them
stagger like a drunken man. –Job 12:25 Nkjv*

NOTES

CHAPTER 4

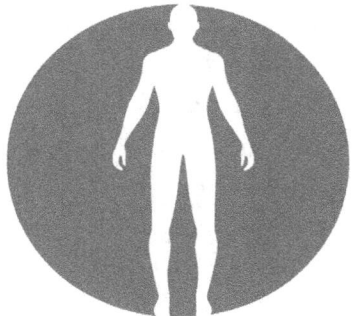

CREATION PERMITTING GOD

"And God said, Let there be light: and there was light."
–Genesis 1:3 KJV

I recall the moment I received the gospel in my spirit; not that I hadn't heard the gospel preached before, but this time it was different; it was as if a light turned on The power and life of that word resonated strongly within my heart, beginning to enlighten the eyes of my darkened understanding. I realized I stood at a crossroads, faced with a choice between light and darkness. Genesis 1:4 tells us that God divided the light from the darkness. Thank God, I chose the light. I could discern the difference between light and darkness, sin and righteousness, good and evil.

The Father, seeing my helplessness, sent His Spirit just as He sent His Spirit to hover over the water. He stirred and activated His Word in the preacher's belly that day about Jesus dying for our sins and just as the earth was renewed (reborn), I was born again. *He that believeth on me as the Scripture has said out of his belly shall flow Rivers of living water (John 7:38).*

Let's delve deeper into this process concerning the earth. God spoke to a ruined earth, saying, *"Let there be light!" (Genesis 1:3)*. First off, let me clarify that the word "let" is permissive—it implies permission. Thus, we see God speaking to His creation, the earth, as He speaks to us, mankind. God is asking his creation to permit him to make a change. let me remind you that the meaning of God's glory is *light* and *splendor*. God is light; it is one of the manifestations of God's glory, and God started with His light. This light was not sourced from the sun or moon, as they had not yet been revealed until the 4th day. Many biblical scholars believe as well as myself that the sun and the moon were created already, but not fully revealed until the fourth day.

As a matter of fact in *The Message Bible* you see GOD saying lights come out!

> *God spoke: "Lights! Come out! Shine in Heaven's sky! Separate Day from Night. Mark seasons and days and years, Lights in Heaven's sky to give light to Earth." And there it was.*
> *–Genesis 1:14-15 MSG*

-In the GNTD Bible you see GOD saying "lights appear"
-In the CEV Bible. You see GOD saying "lights appear"
-In the GNBDC Bible. You see GOD saying "light appear"
-In the NLT Bible. You see GOD saying "lights appear."

> *"And God said, Let there be lights in the firmament of the heaven to divide the day from the night; and let them be for signs, and for seasons, and for days, and years: And let them be for lights in the firmament of the heaven to give light upon the earth: and it was so. And God made two great lights; the greater light to rule the day, and the lesser light to rule the night: he made the stars also. And God set them in the firmament of the heaven to give light upon the earth, [18] And to rule over the day and over the night, and to divide the light from the darkness: and God saw that it was good. [19] And the evening and the morning were the fourth day."*
> *–Genesis 1:14-19 KJV*

The sun and moon could not deliver the earth from spiritual darkness, just as guns, bombs, and missiles cannot deliver you from the power of the enemy. When our Lord illuminated the earth with His glory, I don't believe that only one side of the earth was lit up as it is when the sun shines. Instead, I believe that God's glory illuminated the entire earth—north, south, east, and west—all at once. Here is a biblical example of GOD'S GLORY being light instead of the sun and moon.

"The city had no need of sun or moon to shine on it, for the glory of God gave it light, and its lamp was the Lamb. The nations will walk by its light, and to it, the kings of the earth will bring their treasure. During the day its gates will never be shut, and there will be no night there."–Revelations 21:23

It's evident that God's glory played the role of the sun and moon until they were revealed. God's glory also dealt with spiritual darkness. Genesis 1:3 is a picture of God taking what He was and what was on Him and putting it on the earth—the light of His glory.

"God saw that the light was good, and he separated the light from the darkness." –Genesis 1:4 NIV

Did you catch that? God saw that the light (His glory) was good! He called it good. God's glory was good for the earth. So, being mindful of this paradigm, God's glory is also good for mankind, created from the dust of the ground (the earth). When God's glory came upon His people who were in darkness in Isaiah 60, supernatural increase began to manifest—increase upon increase.

"Arise, shine; for thy light is come, and the glory of the LORD is risen upon thee. For, behold, the darkness shall cover the earth, and gross darkness the people: but the LORD shall arise upon thee, and his glory shall be seen upon thee. And the Gentiles shall come to thy light, and kings to the brightness of thy rising. Lift up thine eyes

roundabout, and see: all they gather themselves together, they come to thee: thy sons shall come from far, and thy daughters shall be nursed at thy side. Then thou shalt see, and flow together, and thine heart shall fear, and be enlarged; because the abundance of the sea shall be converted unto thee, the forces of the Gentiles shall come unto thee. The multitude of camels shall cover thee, the dromedaries of Midian and Ephah; all they from Sheba shall come: they shall bring gold and incense; and they shall shew forth the praises of the LORD. All the flocks of Kedar shall be gathered together unto thee, the rams of Nebaioth shall minister unto thee: they shall come up with acceptance on mine altar, and I will glorify the house of my glory."
–Isaiah 60:1-7 KJV

God is light, glory, splendor, and radiance. When God showed up in the Garden of Eden looking for Adam, He was looking for a reflection (image and likeness) of Himself—His light, His glory, His splendor, His radiance upon Adam and Eve. So in Isaiah 60, we see God taking His glory and placing it upon man—what are the results? We see the start of renewal, replenishing, refreshing, and a new beginning, just as in Genesis 1:2-3—God putting His glory upon the earth. Let's look at Isaiah again.

"The people that walked in darkness have seen a great light: they that dwell in the land of the shadow of death, upon them hath the light shined."
–Isaiah 9:2 King James Version

You notice the Bible says "upon" them. God speaks of His glory resting upon man again, just as it rested upon Adam and Eve initially.

"JESUS answered and said unto him, If a man loves me, he will keep my words: and my FATHER will love him, and WE will come unto him, and make our abode with him."
–St. John 14:23 KJV

There is no separating the Father from His glory. So where God abides, His glory also abides. As Spirit-filled born-again Christians, as we grow by submitting to God, His glory begins to come upon us, resting on us. Isaiah 60:2-3 declares that God promised His light would shine upon us. To truly grasp the depth of this promise, it's vital to understand the full biblical significance of His glory. "Glory" embodies the weightiness, majesty, abundance, magnificence, splendor, wealth, power, radiance, and light of God. It's not something to be satisfied with once experienced; rather, like Moses, we should continuously seek God to reveal His glory to us.

Scripture, such as 2 Timothy 2:1, speaks of our journey from strength to strength, from faith to faith, and from glory to glory, all through the grace of our Lord Jesus Christ. In Isaiah 60:2, we are assured that God's glory will be visible upon us, underscoring the importance of not just experiencing His glory within but also having it manifest upon us.

Moses' encounter with God on Mount Sinai illustrates how prolonged communion with God resulted in His glory resting upon Moses. Such was the intensity of God's presence that Moses's face radiated with divine light, necessitating a veil to shield the people from its brilliance (Exodus 34:29).

God's glory serves another crucial purpose—it scatters darkness. This emphasizes the importance of growing not just in faith but also in God's glory. With His glory upon us, darkness flees wherever we go, just as darkness dispersed before God's glorious light in Genesis 1:3. Unlike natural sunlight, which can cast shadows, God's glorious light leaves no room for darkness to hide.

Today the body of Christ is Awakening to the knowledge of being carriers of God's glory—mobile glory carriers through which his presence shines. As God fills the earth with His glory (Numbers 14:20-21), it's imperative that we, His children, cooperate with His divine plan.

> *Then the Lord said: "I have pardoned, according to your word; but truly, as I live, all the earth shall be filled with the glory of the Lord." –Numbers 14:20-21 NKJV*

In Genesis 1:3, when God speaks, *"Let there be light,"* it reveals a profound truth—that even the Almighty seeks cooperation from His creation. Our willingness to cooperate with God entails agreeing, submitting, and surrendering to His will. This divine dialogue between God and His creation highlights the intimate relationship He desires with us.

Just as God communicated with the earth in the beginning, He continues to speak to us through His creation and His Word. Creation itself bears witness to His existence and glory, as Romans 1:20 emphasizes:

> *For since the creation of the world GOD'S invisible qualities—*
> *HIS eternal power and divine nature—have been clearly seen,*
> *being understood from what has been made,*
> *so that people are without excuse.*
> *–Romans 1:20 NIV*

Moreover, everything in creation works for our good, as Romans 8:28 assures us.

> *And we know that all things work together for good to them*
> *that love GOD, to them who are called according to HIS purpose.*
> *–Romans 8:28 KJV*

Everything God has created is working for us. Yes, the good, the bad, and the ugly are working for your good. For those called according to His purpose, all of creation is working in your favor. Everything on earth, in the stratosphere, and even in the third heaven—God has designed it so that His creation works for your benefit, according to His purpose. This brings to mind the day I got saved, when I permitted, by asking, the Lord to come into my life and be my Lord and Savior. I've come to realize that God doesn't force His creation to accept what was done by Jesus Christ on Calvary. Yes, although the Spirit of God will convict you of sin, righteousness, and judgment, the decision to accept Him as Lord is a personal one.

In John 16:8 (New King James Version), it says, *"And when He has come, He will convict the world of sin, and of righteousness, and of judgment."*

We have to surrender to God and permit an almighty God to deliver us because He has given mankind free will. No matter how messed up your life is, God is waiting for you to ask Him to save you.

Now, let's dive a little deeper. When the Bible says that the Spirit of God was moving upon the face of the waters (Genesis 1:2 KJV), water in the Bible is symbolic of the word of God. Jesus also said that those who believed in Him, that living water (symbolic of the living word of God), would flow out of our bellies like rivers of water (John 7:38 KJV). God was moving upon the face of the waters. Genesis 1:2, is a picture of activation, the spirit of God, stirring, and activating the word. Then immediately we see the word coming forth "Let there be light."

On that point, it's important to note, for us who share the gospel, not to share our favorite message when God opens a door to speak or gives us a platform. Instead, we should deliver a word that has been authorized, empowered, activated, and carries the weight of the Holy Ghost upon it. This living water is what brings about change.

Genesis 1:2-3 is a picture of the Spirit of God (God's power) combined with the Word (Jesus Christ) speaking forth the mind of the Father to the earth **"Let there be light."**

NOTES

NOTES

CHAPTER 5

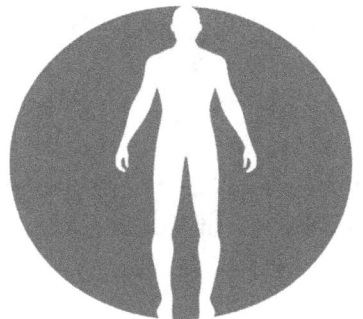

A SEPARATION

And God said, "Let there be a vault between the waters to separate water from water." So God made the vault and separated the water under the vault from the water above it. And it was so. God called the vault "sky." And there was evening, and there was morning—the second day.
–Genesis 1:6-8 (NIV)

In this passage, we witness the divine act of creation, as God, in His infinite wisdom, orchestrates the formation of the heavens and the earth. Prior to the existence of mankind and vegetation, God sets the stage for life on a renewed earth, likened to a woman preparing a nursery for her expected child. It's a breathtaking portrayal of the earth being reborn—a renewal and replenishment orchestrated by the hand of God Himself. God created an atmosphere conducive to life on a renewed earth.

Reflecting on Genesis 1, we're reminded of God's pattern of creating goodness and calling it good. Yet, something occurred between verses one and two that left the earth in darkness, void, and formless. Hence, when God instructs Adam and Eve to "replenish" the earth in

Genesis 1:28, it's not merely about filling it but also about renewing and replacing what was lost.

The imagery of God's glorious light causing a division and separation, banishing spiritual darkness, evokes a profound sense of awe. Imagine a world without shadows, illuminated by the supernatural light of God—a restoration process initiated by the divine hand. As the earth is restored, it basks in the radiance of God's glory. As far as the north, the south, the east and the west, God's glory shone.

Pause for a moment, and allow me to share a personal testimony. After experiencing a spiritual rebirth, I felt a renewing grace upon me, propelling me to grow spiritually. It was a season of peace and spiritual nourishment. It seemed as if there was no warfare for a season, everything seemed peaceful, and if there was any warfare I didn't know it.

Immersed in prayer and the Word, worldly distractions faded away as I focused solely on my relationship with God. Sometimes we're not cooperating and allowing GOD to isolate us so that we can elevate or grow up faster. We hang on to things of the world, and grapple to stay attached to old people, places, and things. All of these would have been distractions from my growth process with the LORD. It was a time of profound transformation—a shedding of old desires and the birth of a new spiritual fervor. A separation from the old.

Indeed, building during times of peace is easier than during times of war, as exemplified by King David's desire to build a house for God. Let me drop this nugget on you.

It's easier to build in a time of peace than war. David a man of war wanted to build GOD a house, but GOD did not allow him.

David said to Solomon: "My son, I had it in my heart to build a house for the Name of the LORD my GOD. But this word of the LORD came to me: 'You have shed much blood and have fought many wars. You are not to build a house for my Name, because you have shed much blood on the earth in my sight."

The LORD told David that his son Solomon (his name meaning peace) was going to build HIM a house.

I'm not saying you cannot build in a time of war, I am saying that it's easier to build in a time of peace. As a matter of fact David stored up for the temple that was to be built by Solomon (so he built up wealth for the building of the temple).

Now getting back to the renewal and replacement, we can learn something valuable here, and that is that GOD'S GLORY (divided) scattered the darkness (spiritual) and then HE began to replace, restore, renew and replenish the earth.

Once I became a born-again believer, my old running buddies began to distance themselves from me. I believe it was because I incessantly talked about my AWESOME GOD. I had a person once tell me that, they meant it as a put down but to me it was a great compliment. As I look back now I realized that my friends hadn't changed but that I had, and for the better. I had become a new creature.

Therefore if anyone is in CHRIST [that is, grafted in, joined to HIM by faith in HIM as SAVIOR], he is a new creature [reborn and renewed by the HOLY SPIRIT]; the old things [the previous moral and spiritual condition] have passed away. -2 Corinthians 5:17 (AMP)

The Bible says in Amos 3:3 can two walk together unless they agree?

I no longer walked in agreement with darkness and the world, but because of the saving grace of GOD and HIS righteousness operating in me, I chose daily to align with GOD's plans, My sin nature (my natural inclination to sin) was gone. I'm not saying that I could not sin but that the desire to sin was no longer there. I love chocolate cake, but it was like I woke up one day and had never tasted chocolate cake before and had no desire to.

The Bible says (JESUS speaking to Peter) when you have been strengthened, strengthen your brethren. Luke 22:32

Don't be shocked when GOD removes certain people out of your life for a season and builds you up spiritually so that you can influence a lost world, and you, not be influenced by a lost world. GOD brought godly people into my life, strong brothers and sisters, knowledgeable in the word and ways of GOD to help me spiritually mature.

THE PARADIGM OF MAN AND EARTH

When JESUS, in Luke 8 (who was invited), went to raise Jairus daughter from the dead, the Bible states HE put a bunch of folks out of the house and brought in several disciples. The atmosphere in that home was shifted by people of faith and *you* also will grow, mature and be shifted by people of faith. JESUS was invited into the house (Jairus cooperating and permitting CHRIST to come in and make changes beside bringing life to his dead daughter).

And, behold, there came a man named Jairus, and he was a ruler of the synagogue: and he fell down at JESUS' feet, and besought HIM that HE would come into his house: for he had one only daughter, about twelve years of age, and she lay a dying. But as HE went the people thronged HIM. And a woman having an issue of blood twelve years, which had spent all her living upon physicians, neither could be healed of any, came behind HIM, and touched the border of HIS garment: and immediately her issue of blood stanched. And JESUS said, Who touched ME? When all denied, Peter and they that were with HIM said, Master, the multitude throng thee and press thee, and sayest thou, Who touched me? And JESUS said, Somebody hath touched ME: for I perceive that virtue is gone out of ME. And when the woman saw that she was not hid, she came trembling, and falling down before HIM, she declared unto HIM before all the people for what cause she had touched HIM, and how she was healed immediately. And HE said unto her, Daughter, be of good comfort: thy faith hath made thee whole; go in peace.

While HE yet spake, there cometh one from the ruler of the synagogue's house, saying to HIM, Thy daughter is dead: trouble not the Master. But when JESUS heard it, HE answered him, saying, Fear not: believe only, and she shall be made whole. And when HE came into the house, HE suffered no man to go in, save Peter, and James, and John, and the father and the mother of the maiden. And all wept, and bewailed her: but HE said, Weep not; she is not dead, but sleepeth. And they laughed him to scorn, knowing that she was dead. And HE

put them all out, and took her by the hand, and called, saying, Maid, arise. And her spirit came again, and she arose straightway: and HE commanded to give her meat. And her parents were astonished: but he charged them that they should tell no man what was done.
—Luke 8:41-56 KJV

We continue to see a separation, when JESUS, the LIGHT of the world, came into the house everything that didn't align with GOD'S will, purpose, and plan for that family and home was put out.

My journey of spiritual growth taught me that God isolates us to elevate us, removing distractions and surrounding us with godly influences. Just as Jesus cleared the house before raising Jairus' daughter, God purges our lives of worldly influences, creating an atmosphere conducive to spiritual growth. Cooperation with God's plan is key—inviting Him into our lives and yielding to His transformative work.

Continuing in Genesis 1, we witness a dialogue between God and His creation, underscoring the importance of cooperation. As God speaks, His creation responds, aligning itself with His divine will. It's a poignant reminder of our role as God's creation—cooperating with His plans for our lives.

And GOD said, Let the waters under the heaven be gathered together unto one place, and let the dry land appear: and it was so. And GOD called the dry land Earth; and the gathering together of the waters called HE Seas: and GOD saw that it was good.
—Genesis 1:9-10 KJV

There are times I wish that GOD would just bust my door down and program me like a robot or put me on a string like a puppet. But, GOD has given us a free will and HE wants us to choose to serve HIM even as HIS creation, just as the earth that had become dark, void and without form cooperated with HIM.

Remember I said earlier that the Bible is made up of patterns, and that GOD speaks in patterns. The story of Cain and Abel further illustrates the contrast between God's ordained approach and man-made religion. Abel's willingness to follow God's pattern stands in stark contrast to Cain's rebellious offering, symbolizing man's tendency to deviate from God's ways.

Abel was willing to follow the pattern that GOD had established showing forth GOD'S Divine plan for man's salvation. Abel, the brother of Cain, was a prophet.

> *Therefore this generation will be held responsible for the blood of all the prophets that has been shed since the beginning of the world, from the blood of Abel to the blood of Zechariah, who was killed between the altar and the sanctuary. Yes, I tell you, this generation will be held responsible for it all.*
> *-Luke 11:50-51*

JESUS said that Abel was a prophet and that settles it. Prophets know the mind of GOD and have an ear for GOD'S voice. Yes I am aware that Abel never uttered a prophecy that was recorded in the Bible. Not all prophets are recorded in the Bible as prophesying verbally. There were those who demonstrated the will and mind of God. We can see such an example In Ezekiel 4, when GOD had Ezekiel to perform such an act or demonstration,

> *Thou also, son of man, take thee a tile, and lay it before thee, and pourtray upon it the city, even Jerusalem: and lay siege against it, and build a fort against it, and cast a mount against it; set the camp also against it, and set battering rams against it round about. Moreover take thou unto thee an iron pan, and set it for a wall of iron between thee and the city: and set thy face against it, and it shall be besieged, and thou shalt lay siege against it. This shall be a sign to the house of Israel. Lie thou also upon thy left side, and lay the iniquity of the house of Israel upon it: according to the number of the days that thou shalt lie upon it thou shalt bear their iniquity.*

For I have laid upon thee the years of their iniquity, according to the number of the days, three hundred and ninety days: so shalt thou bear the iniquity of the house of Israel. And when thou hast accomplished them, lie again on thy right side, and thou shalt bear the iniquity of the house of Judah forty days: I have appointed thee each day for a year. –Ezekiel 4:1-6 KJV

GOD told Ezekiel in verse 3 that it would be for a sign. It was not verbal. I would suggest that you read all of chapter 4. GOD also speaks through Isaiah's demonstration, a sign:

In the year that Tartan came unto Ashdod, (when Sargon the king of Assyria sent him,) and fought against Ashdod, and took it; at the same time spake the LORD by Isaiah the son of Amoz, saying, Go and loose the sackcloth from off thy loins, and put off thy shoe from thy foot. And he did so, walking naked and barefoot. And the LORD said, Like as my servant Isaiah hath walked naked and barefoot three years for a sign and wonder upon Egypt and upon Ethiopia; so shall the king of Assyria lead away the Egyptians prisoners, and the Ethiopians captives, young and old, naked and barefoot, even with their buttocks uncovered, to the shame of Egypt.
–Isaiah 20:1-4 KJV

Cain, Abel's older brother was not willing to bring an animal sacrifice, he was trying to break the pattern, established and ordained by GOD, on how to approach HIM. You're literally seeing a picture of religion where man wants to approach GOD his own way and is not willing to approach GOD the way HE requires. Religion always breaks GOD'S patterns.

And in the process of time it came to pass, that Cain brought of the fruit of the ground an offering unto the LORD. [And Abel, he also brought of the firstlings of his flock and of the fat thereof. And the LORD had respect unto Abel and to his offering: but unto Cain and to his offering he had not respect. And Cain was very wroth, and his countenance fell. And the LORD said unto Cain, Why art thou wroth? and why is thy countenance fallen? If thou doest well, shalt thou not be accepted? and if thou doest not well, sin lieth at the door. And unto thee shall be his desire, and thou shalt rule over him. –Genesis 4:3-7 KJV

Innocent blood was shed to provide a covering for Adam and Eve, they had become aware of their nakedness, no longer clothed with light (Glory). The shedding of blood, a picture of things to come, CHRIST the LAMB of GOD, being our Blood sacrifice for the sins of the world.

So a distinction is clearly made between a GOD-ordained approach and religion (man approaching GOD via his own created pathway). We again see the spirit of religion (doing things man's way) throughout the Bible where men literally begin to build a tower, attempting to approach the heavens in their own way and ability.

4) Then they said, "Come, let us build ourselves a city, with a tower that reaches to the heavens, so that we may make a name for ourselves; –Genesis 11:4 NIV

Throughout history, we see instances of man attempting to reach God through their own efforts, as seen in the construction of the Tower of Babel. Yet, true access to God comes only through Jesus Christ, whose righteousness grants us favor with the Father.

May we, like Abel, embrace God's divine plan, walking in obedience and alignment with His will. And may God deliver us from the spirit of religion, opening our eyes to His truth and guiding us into deeper intimacy with Him.

NOTES

CHAPTER 6

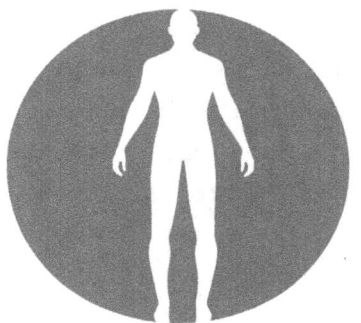

FRUITFUL

And GOD said, Let the earth bring forth grass, the herb yielding seed, and the fruit tree yielding fruit after his kind, whose seed is in itself, upon the earth: and it was so. And the earth brought forth grass, and herb yielding seed after his kind, and the tree yielding fruit, whose seed was in itself, after his kind: and GOD saw that it was good. And the evening and the morning were the third day. –Genesis 1:11-13

Now we literally begin to see the earth becoming productive. Initially, it was a place of no productivity, but it begins to thrive.

Man, when renewed and washed by the shed blood of our LORD and SAVIOR JESUS CHRIST, believing that HE is the son of GOD, growing in knowledge and spirit, becomes useful to GOD, productive in society, fruitful, a valuable asset to the kingdom of GOD.

Let's review the account of day 3 over in Genesis chapter 2.

This is the account of the heavens and the earth when they were created, when the LORD GOD made the earth and the heavens. Now no shrub had yet appeared on the earth and no plant had yet

sprung up, for the LORD GOD had not sent rain on the earth and there was no one to work the ground, but streams came up from the earth and watered the whole surface of the ground.
—Genesis 2:4-6 NIV

GOD, in Gen. Chapter 2, is back tracking. What that means is it's like telling a story and going back to fill in the blanks. HE tells us about the beginning and the first seven days of creation in Gen. Chapter 1, but in Gen. Chapter 2, the LORD decides to point some specific things out from day three.

Remember that when Moses penned the Torah, the first five books of the Bible, he was up on mount Sinai in the PRESENCE of GOD receiving both a download of creation and of the Law. Moses writes what GOD revealed to him, that there were no plants and trees on the earth, there was no such thing as rain, during this time, because the earth would water itself. In the beginning GOD created the earth with the ability to sustain its ground by having water coming up out of the earth and nourish the whole face of the ground. It's a picture of the earth sustaining itself (the ground) by what was released from within the earth. GOD put a watering system in place prior to calling forth the trees, plants, shrubbery, etc.

I don't know if you are getting this picture of what GOD is saying, the moment you ask JESUS CHRIST to be your LORD and SAVIOR and to come into your life, HE fills you with HIS SPIRIT, and the SPIRIT of GOD doesn't come empty-handed but comes bearing wisdom, knowledge, revelation, fruits, and gifts. Again, I remind you the Bible says that we are earthen vessels filled with treasure.

2 Corinthians 4:7 reads, **"But we have this treasure in earthen vessels....**

Just like in the beginning the earth had water treasured on the inside with the ability to sustain itself by what was released from within, in like manner you were created with the ability to water your ground by what you release meaning by what comes up out of your mouth—by the words you speak. When I said water your ground, I am talking about you using what is on the inside of you to make your life productive.

Now let's revisit Adam when GOD granted him dominion over the earth.

> *And God blessed them, and GOD said unto them, Be fruitful, and multiply, and replenish the earth, and subdue it: and have DOMINION over the fish of the sea, and over the fowl of the air, and over every living thing that moveth upon the earth.*
> *–Genesis 1:28 KJV*

Man created in the image and likeness of GOD would, no doubt, be able to manifest GOD-like abilities. At this time he wasn't flawed by sin like we are today but created perfect, He had the nature of GOD and abilities of GOD

Then God said, *"Let us make man in our image, after our likeness: "So GOD created man in HIS own image, in the image of GOD HE created him; male and female HE created them."* –Genesis 1:26–27

Adam, bearing GOD'S image and likeness, would naturally behave like GOD. I am constantly looking at my son's, from their childhood to now being full grown adults and I can identify the traits they have that reminded me of myself.

In Gen. 2 GOD charged Adam to dress the garden,

> *And the LORD God took the man, and put him into the garden of Eden to dress it and to keep it. –Genesis 2:15 KJV*

I believe the picture that pops up in our head is Adam using lawn instruments, but Adam did not have rakes, shovels, a saw and a hoe. The Bible lets us know that Adam didn't break a sweat until he sin, work for Adam was simply speaking, Emulating GOD. GOD was his mentor and teacher. When Adam and Eve sin, creation did not respond to them in the same manner. They had to literally work the ground by the sweat of their brow to get the earth or creation to respond to them.

 THE PARADIGM OF MAN AND EARTH

In Gen 3:17, we see Adam sweating for the first time. To Adam HE said,

"Because you listened to your wife and ate from the tree about which I commanded you, 'You must not eat of it,' "Cursed is the ground because of you; through painful toil you will eat of it all the days of your life. It will produce thorns and thistles for you, and you will eat the plants of the field. By the sweat of your brow you will eat your food until you return to the ground, since from it you were taken; for dust you are and to dust you will return." –Genesis 3:17-19

GOD told Adam, "by the sweat of your brow you will eat your food." Adam would work harder to yield the same results. Adam, prior to sinning operated like his Creator in the garden of Eden; by speaking what he imagined with his mouth. If Adam wanted a certain tree or plant in a certain place he would simply speak it. He had the likeness of GOD, he was created in GOD'S image. Adam descended from speaking to creation to digging holes, planting seeds in the ground, and hand picking the harvest, while sweating from his brow in the heat of the day.

After they (Adam and Eve) fell spiritually, the curse was that his work would be fruitless, difficult, and frustrating. It would require much more effort while the earth naturally would produce thorns and thistles, making things all the more difficult.

According to Gen. 3:17-19, JESUS CHRIST came that through HIM we have authority over creation again, which had been lost through the sin and fall of Adam. But my personal belief is that we are in a gradual process of a turnaround that is coming through the knowledge of who we are and what we possess in and through Christ Jesus.

Again we have our authority through CHRIST JESUS. Through CHRIST we can call (speak) those things that be not as though they are in order to get things done in the earth, according to Romans 4:17.

We can determine things in the earth, especially those things that line up with God's will:

- **Matthew 18:18 King James Bible**

Verily I say unto you, Whatsoever ye shall bind on earth shall be bound in heaven: and whatsoever ye shall loose on earth shall be loosed in heaven.

- **Matthew 18:18 New Living Translation**

I tell you the truth, whatever you forbid on earth will be forbidden in heaven, and whatever you permit on earth will be permitted in heaven.

- **Matthew 18:18 GOD'S WORD® Translation**

I can guarantee this truth: Whatever you imprison, God will imprison. And whatever you set free, God will set free.

- **Matthew 18:18 International Standard Version**

I tell all of you with certainty, whatever you prohibit on earth will have been prohibited in heaven, and whatever you permit on earth will have been permitted in heaven.

When we are positioned in CHRIST HE blesses the work of our hands the same way HE blessed the children of Israel according to Deuteronomy 28:12. The problem is that we are, as GOD'S children, forgetting to include the mouth, or more so the right words.

A man shall eat good by the fruit of his mouth:
–Proverbs 13:2 KJV

This Book of the Law shall not depart from your mouth,
–Joshua 1:8 ESV

How forcible are right words!
–Job 6:25-26 KJV

Remember GOD puts HIS WEIGHT on what HE APPROVES. These types of words become unstoppable. So, you can cancel and even delay GOD'S purpose for your life, by what comes out of your mouth.

A good example of this is when the children of Israel who were only supposed to spend eleven days crossing the wilderness ended up staying in the wilderness for 40 years before crossing into the promised land.

> *There are eleven days' journey from Horeb by the way of mount Seir unto Kadeshbarnea. –Deuteronomy 1:2 NIV*

> *The Israelites had moved about in the wilderness forty years until all the men who were of military age when they left Egypt had died, since they had not obeyed the LORD.*
> *For the LORD had sworn to them that they would not see the land he had solemnly promised their ancestors to give us, a land flowing with milk and honey.*
> *– Joshua 5:6 New International Version*

In Luke 1, GOD sealed up the mouth of Zechariah, the priest, John the Baptist's father to keep him from saying anything detrimental concerning what GOD was purposely doing in the earth.

> *Now while on duty, serving as priest before GOD in the order of his division, As was the custom of the priesthood, it fell to him by lot to enter [the sanctuary of] the temple of the LORD and burn incense. And the whole multitude of the people were praying without at the time of incense. And there appeared unto him an angel of the LORD standing on the right side of the altar of incense. And when Zacharias saw him, he was troubled, and fear fell upon him. But the angel said unto him, Fear not, Zacharias: for thy prayer is heard; and thy wife Elisabeth shall bear thee a son, and thou shalt call his name John. [14] And thou shalt have joy and gladness; and many shall rejoice at his birth. [15] For he shall be great in the sight of the LORD, and shall drink neither wine nor strong drink; and he shall be filled with the HOLY GHOST, even from his mother's womb. [16] And many of the children of Israel shall he turn to the LORD their*

GOD. [17] And he shall go before HIM in the spirit and power of Elias, to turn the hearts of the fathers to the children, and the disobedient to the wisdom of the just; to make ready a people prepared for the LORD. [18] And Zacharias said unto the angel, Whereby shall I know this? for I am an old man, and my wife well stricken in years. [19] And the angel answering said unto him, I am Gabriel, that stand in the presence of GOD; and am sent to speak unto thee, and to shew thee these glad tidings. [20] And, behold, thou shalt be dumb, and not able to speak, until the day that these things shall be performed, because thou believest not my words, which shall be fulfilled in their season. –Luke 1:8-20 AMPC

May the LORD help the body of CHRIST to understand that there is life and death in the power of the tongue.

Life and death are in the power of the tongue.
–Proverbs 18:21

GOD wants to be involved in our everyday affairs, HE wants to put HIS SUPER on our natural. GOD wants to make this journey here on earth a lot more productive and pleasant for HIS people, in the beginning GOD placed man in the GARDEN of Eden which means *Paradise*.

In Matthew 14, the disciples were given an assignment to go to the other side and they hop into a boat and begin to row. The Bible said the ship was in the midst of the sea, tossed with waves: for the wind was contrary. They were struggling trying to get to the other side and JESUS came walking on the sea.

And in the fourth watch of the night JESUS went unto them, walking on the sea. And when the disciples saw HIM walking on the sea, they were troubled, saying, It is a spirit; and they cried out for fear. But straightway JESUS spake unto them, saying, Be of good cheer; it is I; be not afraid.
–Matthew 14:25-27 KJV

The Bible says as soon as they invited CHRIST into the boat they went from struggling to arriving supernaturally at their destination

> *Then they willingly received him into the ship: and immediately the ship was at the land whither they went.*
> *—St. John 6:21*

Note how the disciples went from doing it in their own strength to arriving at their destination through CHRIST JESUS' strength.

WE CAN DO ALL THINGS THROUGH CHRIST WHO STRENGTHENS US, BECAUSE GREATER IS HE THAT IS IN US AND HE THAT IS IN THE WORLD.

Now getting back to you and that weapon under your nose. Did you ever notice in the book of Genesis that the water never stopped coming from out of the earth until man became so degenerate, wicked and sinful that the water ceased from coming out of the ground and changed to instead come from above.

> *The earth also was corrupt before God, and the earth was filled with violence. And God looked upon the earth, and, behold, it was corrupt; for all flesh had corrupted his way upon the earth.*
> *—Genesis 6:11-12 KJV*

> *And the LORD said unto Noah, Come thou and all thy house into the ark; for thee have I seen righteous before me in this generation.*
> *—Genesis 7:1 KJV*

> *For yet seven days, and I will cause it to rain upon the earth forty days and forty nights; and every living substance that I have made will I destroy from off the face of the earth.*
> *—Genesis 7:4 KJV*

The Earth lost its ability to sustain itself, or let me say it this way; it lost the ability to water itself, The life-giving substance that was coming from within. NOW THE GROUND WAS BEING SUSTAINED from what was coming from above, GOD CALLED IT RAIN. And in like manner, man lost his GOD-like ability

Later on in the book of Isaiah GOD would say that HIS word was like rain. Putting us in mind that just as rain sustains the earth, His word sustains us.

As the rain and the snow come down from heaven, and do not return to it without watering the earth and making it bud and flourish, so that it yields seed for the sower and bread for the eater, so is my word that goes out from my mouth: It will not return to me empty, but will accomplish what I desire and achieve the purpose for which I sent it.
—Isaiah 55:10-1 NIV

GOD said HIS word does not come back void meaning fruitless nor empty. God reveals HIMSELF to us by the preaching of the gospel. HE gives us HIS written word to put in our hearts that even as we speak it, declare it, and pray it, it sustains us AS WELL AS BRINGS LIFE TO A DYING PLANET.

When JESUS CHRIST came, HE said that if you believed on HIM that rivers of water would flow up out of you

He that believeth on me, as the scripture hath said, out of his belly shall flow rivers of living water. -John 7:38 KJV -

JESUS is speaking about the WORD of LIFE flowing out of you just like water would flow out of the earth.

Again, keep in mind that we are earthen vessels and that water from a natural perspective is a necessary substance of life besides symbolizing the WORD of GOD in St John 7:38.

You are an earthen vessel, I like to call it an earth suit. You possess a soul, but your true essence is spirit, and your words should be filled with life, not only for yourself but also to bless others.

Through Christ, we not only have the ability to communicate but also to create and reproduce with words. It would be unfair to keep from you the importance of renewing our minds with the word of Almighty GOD and pursuing an intimate relationship with the Holy Spirit. The Holy Spirit guides us to Jesus, who leads us to the Father, and the Father sends the Holy Spirit. The Bible teaches that those who are children of GOD are led by the SPIRIT of GOD (Romans 8:14).

The Bible also says that the tongue is able to set the course of a person's life on fire.

It is the Spirit who gives life; the flesh profits nothing. The words that I speak to you are spirit, and they are life.
–John 6:63 (NKJV)

Jesus said, "the words that I speak they are spirit and they are life." HE called them spiritual words, words that create life. Jesus had the Holy Spirit backing HIS words up. Words authorized by the FATHER.

For I have not spoken on My own authority;
but the FATHER who sent Me gave Me a command,
what I should say and what I should speak
–John 12:49 New King James Version

We are able to open doors and shut doors with words. We are able to dictate to creation with words. We are able to stop storms with words. Jesus did it!

Again, keep in mind that in the garden of Eden, GOD was Adam's mentor. Jesus in the Bible is our mentor or example. HE'S showing us an example of how to live and function on the earth. Remember Jesus took off his glory, and was completely dependent upon the father and the holy spirit.

For you know the grace of our LORD JESUS CHRIST, that though HE was rich, yet for your sakes HE became poor, so that you through HIS poverty might become rich. -2 Corinthians 8:9

Let this mind be in you, which was also in CHRIST JESUS: who, being in the form of GOD, thought it not robbery to be equal with GOD: but made HIMSELF of no reputation, and took upon HIM the form of a servant, and was made in the likeness of men: and being found in fashion as a man, HE humbled HIMSELF, and became obedient unto death, even the death of the cross.
–Philippians 2:5-8 KJV

We see men in the Bible who walk closely with GOD and begin to function like GOD in the earth:

- Elijah stopped the rain for three and a half years. *"Elijah was a human being, even as we are. He prayed earnestly that it would not rain, and it did not rain on the land for three and a half years." –James 5:17 NIV*

- Joshua stopped the orbit of the sun and moon for one full day.

"On the day the LORD gave the Amorites over to Israel, Joshua said to the LORD in the presence of Israel: "Sun, stand still over Gibeon, and you, moon, over the Valley of Aijalon." So the sun stood still, and the moon stopped, till the nation avenged itself on its enemies, as it is written in the Book of Jashar. The sun stopped in the middle of the sky and delayed going down for about a full day. There has never been a day like it before or since, a day when the LORD listened to a human being. Surely the LORD was fighting for Israel!" –Joshua 10:12-14

I am saying that Spirit-filled, Word inspired, Bible-toting, men and women of GOD are dangerous to the kingdom of darkness when we speak life and spiritual words. The spirit realm is the parent realm. The natural realm that we live in was born from the spirit realm when the

LORD spoke His words in Genesis chapter 1. GOD spoke this physical realm into existence.

By the grace of GOD, we too have the ability to allow or stop things in this realm by praying, and decreeing and declaring the right words.

I promise you, God in heaven will allow whatever you allow on earth and God will forbid anything you forbid.

> *I promise that when any two of you on earth agree*
> *about something you are praying for,*
> *my Father in heaven will do it for you.*
> *—Matthew 18:18-22 CEV*

> *How forcible are right words! —Job 6:25 (KJV)*

I like to tell people that they have some influence over the success, joy, and productivity in their lives.

> *"Death and life are in the power of the tongue."*
> *—Proverbs 18:21*

The tongue can be used as either a weapon to harm and destroy or as a tool to build and heal. What kind of impact do your words have in your life and on others?

So, you can participate in dictating the course of your life. The WORD of GOD flowing out of your mouth inspired by the Holy Spirit sustains and impacts you as well as the life of those around you. You can water your ground. There are too many dry Christians walking the earth.

> *Not that which goeth into the mouth defileth a man;*
> *but that which cometh out of the mouth, this defileth a man.*
> *—Matthew 15:11*

> *A man's belly shall be satisfied with the fruit of his mouth;*
> *And with the increase of his lips shall he be filled.*
> *—Proverbs 18:20-21 KJV*

If we only fully understood the power of the tongue and that we were created in GOD'S image and likeness. We are speaking spirits. Again our mouths are for communication, reproduction and creation.

My personal belief is that GOD does us a favor and turns up or down the power in our mouth so that we don't feel the full effect of some of the crazy things that come out of our mouths, until we come to a place of maturity in Christ Jesus.

The children of Israel complained about God, Moses, and Aaron, so much that GOD sent fiery serpent among them. The lesson learned here is that our mouths can get us in trouble as well as bring blessings into our lives.

Then they set out from Mount Hor by the way of the Red Sea, to go around the land of Edom; and the people became impatient because of the journey.

So the people spoke against GOD and Moses: *"Why have you brought us up from Egypt to die in the wilderness? For there is no food and no water, and we are disgusted with this miserable food."*

Then the LORD sent fiery serpents among the people and they bit the people, so that many people of Israel died. So the people came to Moses and said, *"We have sinned, because we have spoken against the LORD and against you; intercede with the LORD, that HE will remove the serpents from us."* And Moses interceded for the people. Then the LORD said to Moses, *"Make a fiery serpent, and put it on a flag pole; and it shall come about, that everyone who is bitten, and looks at it, will live." So Moses made a bronze serpent and put it on the flag pole; and it came about, that if a serpent bit someone, and he looked at the bronze serpent, he lived. Numbers 21:4-9 NASB*

Many born-again Christian, in the body of CHRIST, have not developed a relationship with the Holy Spirit through prayer nor have renewed their minds with the written WORD of GOD, and still speak a fallen degenerate language.

THE PARADIGM OF MAN AND EARTH

For in many things we offend all. If any man offends not in word, the same is a perfect (mature) man, and able also to bridle the whole body. Behold, we put bits in the horses' mouths, that they may obey us; and we turn about their whole body. Behold also the ships, which though they be so great, and are driven of fierce winds, yet are turned about with a very small helm, whithersoever the governor listeth. Even so the tongue is a little member, and boasteth great things. Behold, how great a matter a little fire kindleth! And the tongue is a fire, a world of iniquity: so is the tongue among our members, that it defileth the whole body, and setteth on fire the course of nature; and it is set on fire of hell. For every kind of beasts, and of birds, and of serpents, and of things in the sea, is tamed, and hath been tamed of mankind: But the tongue can no man tame; it is an unruly evil, full of deadly poison. Therewith bless we GOD, even the FATHER; and therewith curse we men, which are made after the similitude of GOD. Out of the same mouth proceedeth blessing and cursing. My brethren, these things ought not so to be. Doth a fountain send forth at the same place sweet water and bitter?
–James 3:2-11

Now you're probably wondering why I continue to use the word degenerate. Let's look at the definition.

Degenerate:

1. Having lost the physical, mental, or moral qualities considered normal and desirable; showing evidence of decline. "a degenerate form of a higher civilization"

2. Lacking some property, order, or distinctness of structure previously or usually present. an immoral or corrupt person. To decline or deteriorate physically, mentally, or morally, "their quality of life had degenerated."

So not only did mankind through Adam fall from the state that GOD created them, but their language fell also or the way they spoke fell. We see Adam immediately saying to GOD that he was afraid.

> *And the LORD GOD called unto Adam, and said unto him, Where art thou? And he said, I heard thy voice in the garden, and I was afraid, because I was naked; and I hid myself. And HE said, Who told thee that thou wast naked?*
> *—Genesis 3:9-12 King James Version*

Unmarred by sin, they were a mirror of the Divine, endowed with the very essence and capabilities of God Himself. This original blueprint serves as a testament to the limitless possibilities of God's creation.

However after he sinned, Adam's behavior towards God underwent a transformation. Have you ever noticed how, when we sin, our demeanor towards God shifts? We no longer feel worthy. We hesitate to step into His presence. We feel a chasm growing between us and God. Before the fall into sin, our prayers and conversations with God are filled with confidence. We decree, declare, and speak boldly, approaching the throne with assurance. However, after stumbling and missing the mark, the enemy comes to make us feel condemned and unworthy.

This narrative reminds us of the original magnificence bestowed upon humanity. It beckons us to strive towards reclaiming that initial state of grace, encouraging us to mend our ways and restore our bond with the Almighty, thereby unlocking the boundless potential within.

NOTES

CHAPTER 7

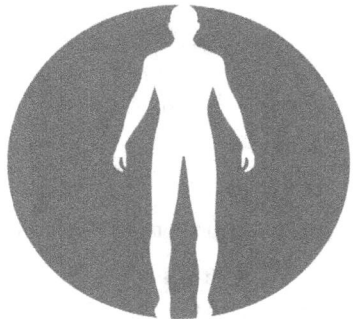

EXPOSURE

And God said, "Let the water under the sky be gathered to one place, and let dry ground appear." And it was so. God called the dry ground "land," and the gathered waters he called "seas." And God saw that it was good.
–Genesis 1:9-10 NIV

The dry land was covered up, and the water in this passage of scripture is a picture of affliction. Isaiah 43:2 confirms that water, sometimes in the Bible, is figurative or symbolic of affliction.

"When you pass through the waters, I will be with you; and when you pass through the rivers, they will not sweep over you. When you walk through the fire, you will not be burned; the flames will not set you ablaze." –Isaiah 43:2 NIV

"Now therefore, behold, the Lord bringeth up upon them the waters of the river, strong and many, even the king of Assyria, and all his glory: and he shall come up over all his channels, and go over all his banks: ..." –Isaiah 8:7-10 NIV

THE PARADIGM OF MAN AND EARTH

GOD is going to expose things that have been hidden and covered up in the earth. Just like the land that was hidden/covered by the sea did not start in a state of not being seen, it could not be seen until GOD commanded the sea to uncover it, by saying *"let it appear."*

It was never intended to be covered by the sea, this was something that was done by Satan and his destructive nature spoken of earlier in the book which caused the Earth to be empty of life, flooded, covered by the sea, and unable to show it's true form and design. It is the reason why we see God telling Adam And Eve in Genesis 1:28 to refill the Earth. God called it dry ground, Putting you in mind of a ground that is moisture free completely separated. A separation between the sea and the Earth. No mixtures. Even creating an unseen border between the Sea and land.

One of the problems in the body of Christ is that there has been a lot of mixtures concerning the church where it's hard to tell the difference between the real and unreal. The genuine and the non genuine.

GOD is bringing forth what's good for society, the world needs to see the **real church**, something that the enemy Satan has worked hard to cover up. Also, GOD is bringing forth things covered up and hidden within you. You are GOD'S earthen tabernacle. Additionally, things hidden in the body of CHRIST, the enemy will not be able to cover them up.

The world needs to see us, let me say it this way, the world needs to see GOD'S light, POWER, HEALING which is hidden in you. Things that we do not know of...

The LORD is bringing it forth.

I heard the LORD say exposure in the early parts of 2024, but everything you see might not be a true exposure. The enemy is good at twisting the truth, and diverting from a true exposure, he knows a little of what GOD wants to do in this season because GOD doesn't do anything unless HE first reveals it to HIS prophets, who announces it in the earth.

> **Surely the LORD GOD will do nothing, but HE revealeth HIS secret unto HIS servants the prophets. –Amos 3:7**

The enemy (satan) will attempt to create what looks like exposure but is not in order to divert from the real exposure and every exposure is not going to be a bad thing.

There will be good exposure and there will be bad exposure.

It's time to see what's in you.

It's time for the world to see GOD within you.

GOD is going to expose you to the world, so that the world can see what's in you.

FATHER, expose the children of light.

NOTES

CHAPTER 8

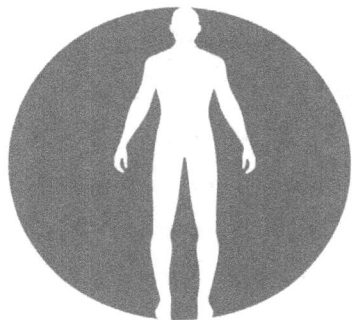

THE PRAYER

I want to encourage you to begin to *pray* Genesis chapter 1, verse 1 through 14 and encourage you to *meditate* on it so that you may grasp the powerful revelations and truth concerning this passage of scripture in the Bible.

LET US PRAY:`

Almighty GOD who has created the heavens and the earth,
even mankind. FATHER just as the earth was void,
without form and full of darkness.
It is the state of mankind on the earth.
Father we need your GLORY and the light of your GLORY.
We need LIGHT that we might arise and shine,
that we might be able to get up out of obscurity and darkness
and come to your marvelous light.
FATHER stir up a mighty word in the belly of your people even
as the spirit of GOD moves across the face of the water, stirring it.
Stir it in the belly of your preachers and even lay members,

*so that it might run up out of their bellies
like running rivers of water.
For your words says, "the harvest is plentiful but the laborers
are few." FATHER, stir up your word by your SPIRIT, and let
there be light in the hearts of your people understanding.
Give to them a spirit of wisdom and revelation
in the knowledge of you.
Convict the sinner by your SPIRIT
of sin, righteousness and judgment
when they hear the word of GOD preached.
Let the light of YOUR word divide the truth from the darkness
and cause them to realize that they're at a crossroad of decision.
Grant them a willing spirit, even as David prayed in Psalms
51 for a free and willing spirit. Free up your people's will to make
a decision to serve you all the days of their lives.
And FATHER, even as you created an atmosphere
that was conducive to life, create an atmosphere that's conducive
to the life of those that you are saving.
Send strong and faithful people into the lives of born again
men, women, and children of GOD that they might mature
and grow according to your will.
And FATHER even as you cause the afflicting waters to flow
back off of the land. My prayer is that you would bring about a
separation, separate and remove things (bondages and soul ties),
and godless people out of the lives of those who are freshly born-
again that they might grow to complete maturity and be fruitful
and bring forth fruit in the earth. That they might be the salt of
the earth in Jesus' name. Amen.*

ABOUT THE AUTHOR

Pastor Thomas Robinson, Jr.

Dr. Thomas grew up as a member of Zion Orthodox Primitive Baptist Church in Cocoa, Fl. As a member there for 25 years, he established a great biblical foundation under the leadership of Reverend P.L. Jones.

Dr. Thomas then became a member of New Hope Deliverance Temple at the age of 28 and spent 17 years growing in ministry and leadership roles under the tutelage of Pastor C.L. Carter. During this time, he spent 11 years doing nursing home and 'Good News' jail and prison ministry, serving as chaplain assistant at the local prison and jail in Sharpes, Florida. Under Pastor Carter's leadership, Dr. Thomas accepted his call to ministry and was ordained during this time.

In 1994, Dr. Thomas received an AA degree from Brevard Christian College and went on to receive a Bachelor of Arts from Jacksonville Theological Seminary in 1996.

Dr. Thomas became the senior pastor of Mainstream International Ministries in 2008 during which time he spent many years doing radio and television broadcasting. He went on to become pastor of Victory international Praise Ministries in 2017, which he now functions as an overseer under the leading of the Holy Spirit.

Dr. Thomas has been married to Dr. Teresa Robinson for 34 years and has 2 sons, who also function in ministry alongside him.

YOU WRITE, WE PUBLISH, TOGETHER WE CREATE...

DIVINE WORKS PUBLISHING, LLC.

A co-publishing service for indie authors seeking a strategic bigger partner alliance for greater visibility and success in today's overcrowded marketplace.

www.DivineWorksPublishing.com

561-990-BOOK (2665)
info@DivineWorksPublishing.com

www.ingramcontent.com/pod-product-compliance
Lightning Source LLC
Chambersburg PA
CBHW050042080526
44586CB00014B/1420